NEW
RESOLUTION

Understanding Mental Resilience and Breaking the Chains of Addiction.

GODWIN GEORGE

ISBN: 9798870193526
Imprint: Independently published

DEDICATION

This Book is Dedicated to God Almigty andt to our New granddaughter Jenik Mary Ayuba.

CONTENTS

ACKNOWLEDGMENTS

I Thank God Almighty for His Mercy over my Life and Family.   My warmth acknowledgment goes to   the entire family of late. Mr. Judge Gumi.

CHAPTER ONE
Introduction

There are many reasons why people drink alcohol and take drugs. Some use these substances to help them to relax, to feel more lively, to feel less inhibited or to feel pleasure. Some the effects of these substances make it seem easier to cope with life challenges. Some use substances for religious reasons or to fit in with the crowd. Others may be curious about the effects of a specific drug. Whichever reason, every substance has an effect on the body system, either positive or negative effect. The brain is the major organ that produce or response to the actions on these substances. When we talk of substance addiction, we mostly think of the chemical-based factors that compel someone to use such substance which is marked by increased tolerance i.e. needing more to get the same effect. But not everyone with the problem of substance use manifest such physical signs of addiction. People who are not chemically dependent can also struggle with cravings, mental obsessions, or other compulsive behaviors that can lead to relapse. Studies have shown that the brain can over time hijack one's sense of control, perhaps because of damage to certain brain receptors as a result of the effect exerted on the brain by those substances. In order to understand addiction better, neuroscientists are also investigating the highly complex interactions among the brain's reward and control systems; and studying how behaviors are influenced not only by chemicals but by habit, repetition and reinforcement.

Definition of Addiction

Addiction is the repetitive and compulsive use of a substance despite its harmful consequences, with or without chemical dependence. It is also defined as a chronic, relapsing brain disease that is characterized by compulsive drug seeking and use, despite harmful consequences. It is considered a brain disease because drugs change the brain structure and how its function. These brain changes can be long-lasting, and can lead to the harmful behaviors seen in people who abuse substances.

People with problem of addiction or substance use mostly suffer from underlying or untreated psychiatric or psychological problems such as depression, anxiety, Post Traumatic Syndrome Disorder (PTSD) bipolar disorder etc. Addiction can manifest as:

- Recurrent substance use resulting in a failure to fulfill major role obligations at work, school, or home (e.g., repeated absences or poor work performance related to substance use; substance-related absences, suspensions, or expulsions from school; neglect of children or household).

- Recurrent substance use in situations in which it is physically hazardous (e.g., driving an automobile or operating a machine when impaired by substance use).

- Recurrent substance-related legal problems (e.g., arrests for substance-related disorderly conduct).

- Continued substance use despite having persistent or recurrent social or interpersonal problems caused or exacerbated by the effects of the substance (e.g., arguments with spouse about consequences of intoxication, physical fights).

Addiction is more like other diseases, such as heart disease. Both disrupt the normal, healthy functioning of the underlying organ, and have serious harmful consequences, and are also preventable and treatable, but if left untreated, can last a lifetime.

CHAPTER TWO
Substance and Behavioral Addiction

Addiction is a complex and pervasive issue that can manifest in various forms, affecting individuals across diverse demographics. Substance addiction, involving the misuse of drugs or alcohol, and behavioral addiction, characterized by compulsive engagement in certain activities, share commonalities while presenting unique challenges Substance addiction involves the compulsive use of substances, such as drugs or alcohol, despite adverse consequences. It often results in physical and psychological dependence, making it difficult for individuals to quit. Substance abuse alters brain chemistry, affecting neurotransmitters like dopamine, which play a vital role in reward and pleasure. Over time, individuals may develop tolerance, requiring increased amounts to achieve the same effects. Withdrawal symptoms can be severe, reinforcing continued substance use. Common Substances: Alcohol, Opioids, Stimulants and Sedatives.

Alcohol

Alcohol is a natural substance formed by the reaction of fermenting sugar with yeast spores. Although there are many alcohols, the kind in alcoholic beverages is known scientifically as ethyl alcohol and chemically as C_2H_5OH. Its abbreviation, EtOH, is sometimes seen in medical records and in various other documents and publications. By strict definition, alcohol is classified as a food because it contains calories; however, it has no nutritional value. Different alcoholic beverages are produced by using different sources of sugar for the fermentation process. For example, beer is made from malted barley, wine from grapes or berries, whiskey from malted grains, and rum from molasses. The alcohol content varies by type of beverage. For example, most American beers contain 3 to 6 percent alcohol, wines average 10 to 20 percent, and distilled beverages range from 40 to 50 percent alcohol. The average sized drink, regardless of beverage, contains a similar amount of alcohol. That is, 12 ounces of beer, 3 to 5 ounces of wine, and a cocktail with 1 ounce of whiskey all contain approximately 0.5 ounce of alcohol. If consumed at the same rate, they all would have an equal effect on the body. Alcohol exerts a depressant effect on the brain, resulting in behavioral and mood changes. The effects of alcohol on the brain are proportional to the alcoholic concentration in the blood. Most states consider that an individual is legally intoxicated with a blood alcohol level of 0.08 to 0.10 percent. The body burns alcohol at the rate of about 0.5 ounce per hour, so behavioral changes would not be expected to occur in an individual who slowly consumed only one averaged-sized drink per hour. Alcohol is thought to have a more profound effect when an individual is emotionally stressed or fatigued (National Institute on Alcohol Abuse and Alcoholism [NIAAA], 2000).

Drugs

Drugs are most commonly abusive substance, regardless of the chemical effect it exerts on the vital organs of the body. Drugs have both therapeutic effect and adverse effect. About 80% of the drug effects are Therapeutic in nature while 20% are poisonous to the body. Most abused drugs produce intense feelings of pleasure. This initial sensation of euphoria is followed by other effects, which differ with the type of drug used. For example, with stimulants such as cocaine, the "high" is followed by feelings of power, self-confidence, and increased energy. In contrast, the euphoria caused by opiates such as heroin is followed by feelings of relaxation and satisfaction. However, drugs can quickly take over a person's life. Over time, if drug use continues, other pleasurable activities become less pleasurable, and taking the drug becomes necessary for the user just to feel "normal." They may then compulsively seek and take drugs even though it causes tremendous problems for themselves and their loved ones. Some people may start to feel the need to take higher or more frequent doses, even in the early stages of their drug use. Even relatively moderate drug use poses dangers. Consider how a social drinker can become intoxicated, get behind the wheel of a car, and quickly turn a pleasurable activity into a tragedy that affects many lives.

Behavioral Addiction

Behavioral addiction pertains to compulsive engagement in certain activities despite negative consequences. Unlike substance addiction, it does not involve the ingestion of substances but centers on behavioral patterns. Activities like gambling, gaming, or shopping activate the brain's reward system, releasing dopamine and reinforcing the behavior. Individuals with behavioral addiction often struggle to control their impulses, leading to excessive time and energy devoted to the addictive behavior. Common Behaviors such as Gambling, Gaming, Internet use and Shopping.

Gambling

Today, many have risked their lives and properties to gambling. Gambling has emerged as one of the simple and easiest but difficult means of getting money. As such many often has lost lives and properties to gambling. Indications that a person is experiencing addiction to gambling include the sheer amount of the gambling activity, the person is concern about its excessiveness, the strength of desire for and preoccupation with gambling, a feeling of loss of control, and economic, social and psychological harms. Those harms include debt, poor work performance and loss of employment, criminality (especially theft, fraud and embezzlement), marital and family disharmony and separation, stress-related physical symptoms, and depression and attempted and completed suicide. Studies have shown that the most troublesome addictions in the near future could be the forms of gambling and other types of consumption that combine certain features such as:

- Easy availability, particularly when opportunities are so many that they become part of national life, such as gambling machines in pubs and shopping malls and gambling via personal computers.

- Rapidly achieved, intense emotional reward.

- The opportunity for continuous play or a rapid return to play. The liability of addiction will be enhanced by features that add to the entrapment potential of the activity, such as betting on the same numbers, having an illusion of control, believing that one is nearly winning or is improving performance, or getting to know other participants, perhaps in an Internet chat room.

Activities that could carry greatest future risks of behavioral addiction include: Gambling machines, Gambling on Internet sites, Pornography on the Internet, Internet games, chat rooms, Shopping and Eating etc. **Sexuality** Sexual addiction, also known as hyper-sexuality or compulsive sexual behavior, it is characterized by an individual's inability to control or resist their sexual impulses, leading to negative consequences in various aspects of life. Like other forms of addiction, it can impact relationships, work, and overall well-being. Sexuality is a fundamental aspect of the human experience, but for some individuals, it can evolve into a relentless and compulsive force. Sexual addiction goes beyond healthy sexual exploration and becomes a disruptive force in the lives of those affected.

Sexual addiction is not officially recognized as a mental health disorder in diagnostic manuals like the DSM-5, but it is widely acknowledged in the field of psychology.

Sexual addiction is not officially recognized as a mental health disorder in diagnostic manuals like the DSM-5, but it is widely acknowledged in the field of psychology. The origins of sexual addiction are multifaceted and often interconnected with psychological, biological, and environmental factors. Traumatic experiences, such as childhood abuse or neglect, can contribute to the development of sexual addiction. Additionally, neurobiological factors and an individual's upbringing may play crucial roles in shaping their relationship with sex.

Excessive time spent on sexual activities, neglect of responsibilities, and the inability to stop engaging in such behaviors despite negative consequences are common signs of sexual addiction. The repercussions of sexual addiction can extend beyond the individual, impacting relationships, professional life, and mental health. Feelings of guilt, shame, and isolation are often prevalent. Treatment often involves therapy, support groups, and addressing underlying psychological factors. It's essential to approach the topic with empathy, recognizing that individuals struggling with sexual addiction may require professional help to manage and overcome their challenges. In conclusion, substance and behavioral addiction share common traits rooted in the brain's reward system. Recognizing the similarities and differences between the two is crucial for developing effective prevention and treatment strategies. A holistic approach that combines medical interventions, psychotherapy, and support networks offers the best chance for individuals to overcome the challenges posed by addiction.

CHAPTER THREE
Manifestations of Addiction

Just like any other disease, addiction to substance or drugs also shows some physical, behavioral and emotional signs. It is very delicate to understand that these manifestations are not ordinary. They occur as a result of the effect exerted on the brain by drugs or substance, which changes the functional and structural part of the brain. The brain reward and pleasure system is affected, and the result is the manifestation seen in people who are addicted to drugs or substance, either physically, behaviorally or emotionally. Long-term effect can also have an overall impact on health, leading to liver cirrhosis or damage as a result of excessive alcohol or toxic drug intoxication, immunological dysfunction and respiratory problems. It is important we consider these manifestations accordingly for early detection and intervention.

PHYSICAL MANIFESTATION

Withdrawal Syndrome: This syndrome is a physical indication on substance dependence or drug addiction, which occur in an attempt to quit. This manifest with symptoms such as Nausea, Vomiting, Sweating, fatigue and increased heart rate. The individual manifest these symptoms when trying to stop consumption of addictive substance.

Tremor (Shakes): This symptom manifest especially in the hands and legs.

This is because the body becomes dependent on a substance and the absence of that substance or drugs will trigger the involuntary movements of the muscle. This is as a result of the effect on the psycho-motor domain of the brain.

Hygiene: Individuals entangled with addiction often neglect personal hygiene. They have poor hygienic practice and grooming habits, unkempt appearance and self-care deficit. All these are common physical manifestations of addiction coupled with substance dependence.

Sleep Disturbances: The physiology of sleep is affected. This is a common diagnosis in Nursing care plan known as "Altered sleep pattern". Substance abuse can lead to insomnia or, conversely, excessive sleeping. These changes often result from the impact of drugs or alcohol on the central nervous system, affecting the body's natural sleep-regulating mechanisms (Sleep-wake cycle).

Weight Imbalance: People grappling with addiction experience unexplained weight changes. Addiction can cause significant shifts in appetite, leading to either rapid weight loss or gain. This may be attributed to altered metabolism, nutritional deficiencies, or changes in eating habits associated with substance use. For example, Alcohol has no nutritional value, consuming it will neither increase or reduce weight but inversely affect appetite.

Long-term effect on health: Chronic substance abuse affects the overall health status of an individual. Depending on the substance has a long-term effect which may cause damage to the liver, respiratory dysfunctions, immune compromise, and cardiovascular issues later in life. Hence, there's a need for health awareness regarding long term effect of drug or substance dependence.

BEHAVIORAL DEVIATIONS

Manifestation of addiction extends beyond just the physical indicators. There are behaviors exhibited by individuals suffering with substance addiction and these behaviors give insights into the depth of their dependency on substance. Knowing these behaviors early will help in prompt intervention, support and rehabilitation. These are:

Social withdrawal/relationship strain: Interpersonal relationships can strain and leads to social withdrawal and isolation, resulting in diminishing interest in maintaining social connections and neglect of relationships, then withdrawal from activities that were once enjoyed with others. The addiction becomes a focal point, overshadowing interpersonal bonds.

Risk-Taking Behavior: There's a visible increase in risk-taking behavior, in which the substance addicted individuals may disregard personal safety and engage in activities that pose a threat to themselves and others. They neglect friendly advice and sees every decision as good and pleasant.

Tolerance and Escalation: As addiction progresses, individuals often develop tolerance, requiring increasing amounts of the substance or engagement in the behavior to achieve the desired effect. This escalation is reflected in behavioral patterns, where what was once a moderate and controlled indulgence transforms into a compulsive and all-encompassing pursuit.

Compulsion and Ritualism: Behaviors associated with addiction often become compulsive and ritualistic. There's a need to always engage in a repetitive and predictable pattern of action or use of substance despite harmful consequence. Everything seem normal to them. Interference or denial will lead to withdrawal and social isolation.

Altered Routine and Priorities: There's a shift in daily routines and change in priorities. Individuals may alter their schedules to accommodate the demands of their addiction, with activities like work, family responsibilities, and social engagements taking a back seat to the pursuit of the addictive substance. Examples are: Staying awake all night, Desperate to make phone calls at 4 a.m. or seeing phone calls at odd hours, not attending school, work or going in late and Loss of job.

EMOTIONAL OR PSYCHOLOGICAL INDICATIONS

The emotional repercussions of addiction are readily apparent and equally profound. Addiction to substance or drugs affects the cognitive/psychological domain of an individual which express itself in emotion instability. There's emotional withdrawal from friends, family and social activities to emotionally avoid judgment and protect personal secrets. This exacerbate emotional distress and foster perpetuation of addictive behaviors.

Irritability and Mood Swings (Bipolar affective disorder): The presence of mood swings and unexplained irritability are pervasive alteration in emotions that are manifested by Depression and Mania or both. Addicted Individual with mood swing can sometimes be happy or sad, sometimes nothing interests them. This is evident that substance either harmful or not, affect the brain reward system.

Anxiety and depression can be both a cause and a consequence of addiction. Substance abuse can temporarily alleviate these emotional struggles, but in the long run, it often exacerbates them, contributing to a dual challenge for those seeking recovery. Individuals may lose interest in activities they once found enjoyable. Hobbies, relationships, and personal goals take a back seat as the focus shifts more intensely towards obtaining and using the addictive substance. This emotional disengagement can lead to a sense of emptiness and loss.

There's also a problem of denial. Individuals may become defensive when confronted about their substance use, creating emotional barriers that hinder open communication. This defensive behavior is often a protective mechanism to shield the addicted individual from scrutiny. Temporal euphoria induced by substance use gives way to emotional crashes during periods of abstinence or attempts to quit. These extreme emotional fluctuations underscore the emotional turbulence inherent in addiction.

Addiction is a condition that can be successfully treated and managed. Relapses, however, can and do occur. Given this, people with substance use problems need to have information on how to find treatment, and how to use periods when substance use is not a problem to preserve their health and avoid relapse. This information can also help family members support their relative or partner.

Research shows that more than half of people with substance use disorders have also had mental health problems, especially anxiety or depression, sometime in their lifetime (Reiger et al., 1990). The relationship between substance use and mental health problems is complex. Some people with mental health problems use substances to help themselves feel better, but end up making the situation worse. When people have mental health problems, even limited substance use (e.g., a drink or two) can worsen the problems. There is hope for recovery, though, it is a journey, sometimes a long one. It takes courage and determination to deal with substance use problems, but as the saying goes "Prevention is better than cure". Addiction to substance is best by first reducing and avoiding substance use.

CHAPTER FOUR
Implications of Addiction

CRAVING

Substance Craving is a motivational state of persistent drug seeking behavior. It is considered as one of the main features of substance use disorders in the new DSM-V classification. Drug or Substance craving is an intense desire to use substances that one was previously addicted to. It typically occurs after exposure to the substance of addiction which reminds an individual of the addiction, or causes unwanted emotions that makes one to use the drugs or alcohol. These cravings, or uncontrollable desire to use drugs or take alcohol, can come with little or no warning and its usually very powerful. Substance craving can be very strong and intimidating, not dangerous but normal. It can make an individual feel as though he/she won't get better until he/she consume the substance. Cravings are the direct implication of the alteration in the brain, which occur as a result of the effect exerted by the substance of addiction. The brain reward system begins associating the feeling of pleasure registered by the substance as a result of repetitive use, causing the body to get use of it even when deprived. As an individual attempt to quit the addicted substance, the brain goes into overdrive as it attempts to reach normal functioning without the substance it has become dependent on. Withdrawal syndrome is a manifestation of this brain chemistry. Craving is extremely common among people in convalescence phase. Though it can vary in strength, frequency and duration.

The longer the period of addiction, the worse the craving become. The more severe the addiction, the greater the alteration in the brain chemistry, which affect mood, emotion, thought and decision-making process. Craving gets more severe in the first 1-3 weeks after quitting drugs or alcohol, though less tense. It can also be intermediate depending on the timer per day, external trigger and or mood.

TOLERANCE

Tolerance is when the body and brain adapt to the presence of a substance, requiring increasing amounts to achieve the same desired effect. This phenomenon can occur with various substances, including drugs, alcohol, and prescription medications. It is the diminishing response to a substance over time, leading individuals to need higher doses to experience the same effects. This is a complex process involving neurobiological changes in the brain's receptors and neurotransmitter systems. The development of tolerance is often linked to adaptations in the central nervous system. Repeated exposure to a substance can lead to alterations in neurotransmitter release, receptor sensitivity, and other neurobiological processes. These changes contribute to the decreased responsiveness to the substance. As individuals develop tolerance, they may increase their substance intake, putting them at a higher risk of dependence and addiction. This escalating pattern of use can lead to severe physical and psychological consequences. It is closely associated to physical dependence, where the body acquaint to the presence of the substance and experiences withdrawal symptoms when it is absent. The development of tolerance often precedes the onset of dependence, further complicating the addiction cycle. It can also influence treatment strategies; as higher doses of medications may be needed for individuals with opioid or alcohol tolerance. Additionally, managing tolerance is a consideration when tapering off certain substances during the detoxification process. Substance tolerance is a significant factor in the development and progression of addiction. Understanding the neurobiological mechanisms behind tolerance is very important for developing effective prevention and treatment strategies to address the complex challenges of substance use disorder.

WITHDRAWAL SYNDROME

As earlier explained in the previous chapter, withdrawal occur when an individual attempt to quit substance addiction and manifest with signs and symptoms such as Nausea, Vomiting, Sweating etc. It also has some psychological symptoms such as Mood swing, Irritability, Cravings etc. It is the set of physical and psychological symptoms that occur when a person who is dependent on a substance suddenly reduces or stops its use. Withdrawal symptoms can vary widely depending on the substance involved, the duration of use, and individual differences. Common substances associated with withdrawal include alcohol, opioids, heroin, cannabis and stimulants. The duration and severity of withdrawal symptoms vary widely. In some cases, symptoms may start within a few hours of the last substance use and peak within a few days. For others, withdrawal may be a more prolonged process lasting weeks or even months. The severity of withdrawal can also range from mild discomfort to life-threatening conditions, particularly in cases involving substances like alcohol or benzodiazepines. In management of withdrawal, in some cases, medical supervision is required. Certain medications can be used to ease withdrawal symptoms and reduce cravings, promoting a more comfortable recovery. Behavioral therapies are essential in addressing the psychological aspects of withdrawal, helping individuals develop coping strategies and prevent relapse. However, support groups can provide a sense of community affirmation and understanding the patient/client during the challenging withdrawal period. The challenge of withdrawal is formidable for individuals in convalescence period of addiction. Recognizing the signs, seeking appropriate support, and implementing comprehensive treatment strategies are crucial steps in navigating this complex and often difficult phase.

RELAPSE

As much as management and treatment progresses, there's hope for recovery, rehabilitation and or total return to normal self and good sense of humor. However, if this is not successfully achieved, then the return to substance use or engaging in addictive behaviors after a period of abstinence or successful treatment is inevitable. This is called relapse. It is a common and often challenging aspect of the recovery process, and individuals struggling with addiction may experience relapse for various reasons. Some individuals may believe they have gained enough control over their addiction, leading to a sense of overconfidence. This can result in neglecting self-care and treatment activities, making relapse more likely. Also, associating with individuals who continue to use substances or engage in addictive behaviors can exert considerable pressure, making it challenging to maintain sobriety. It is important to understand that addiction causes structural and functional changes in the brain, impacting decision-making and impulse control. Even after periods of abstinence, these changes may persist, making an individual more vulnerable. Physical and psychological withdrawal symptoms can be powerful triggers for relapse. Effective management of withdrawal symptoms is essential during the early stages of recovery. In management and addressing relapse in addiction, a comprehensive approach of ongoing support, therapy, education, and the development of coping strategies are very crucial. Also, recognizing warning signs early and having a solid relapse prevention plan in place are essential components of a successful recovery.

CHAPTER FIVE
Role of Mental Resilience in Addiction Recovery

Adversity and stress can come in the shape of family or relationship problems, health problems, or school and financial worries, among others. In addiction recovery, resilience is one's ability to bounce back from a negative experience with competent functioning. Resilience plays a vital role for an individual in convalescence phase. People who suffer from addiction and are in recovery phase, need to understand mental resilience in order to build strong capability in overcoming the chains of addiction and its relapse.

Resilience is a key factor in protecting and promoting good mental health, it is an individual's ability to successfully adapt to life tasks in the face of social disadvantage or highly adverse conditions. Studies has shown that resilience has an important role in the prevention of substance use, and those with tendency to addiction are less prone to substance use because of the ability to deal with difficult situations and flexible response to the challenges of daily life. It is an ongoing process of meaning-making and growth in which the only reliable constant is the mutually dependent capacity of the individual and their environment for change. It also captures how people not only survive a variety of challenging circumstances, but thrive in the face of such adversity.

The way people behave is shaped by a range of factors including personality and past experience, as well as current circumstances and the people around us. All of these things therefore influence a person's resilience. This is why resilience play a vital role in addiction recovery phase, to help sustain good mental health after the cycle of addiction.

IMPORTANCE OF RESILIENCE

Research suggests that the ability to cope well under pressure is based on a positive outlook, combined with strategies to manage pressure. In addiction recovery, resilience helps:

- Understand and value the meaning of what do at work.
- Coping in relationship with the people around.
- Taking a problem-solving approach to difficulty.
- Keeping a sense of perspective (and humor) when things goes wrong.
- Being flexible and willing to adapt to change and to learn.
- Greeting new situations, new people and new demands with a positive attitude.
- Drawing on a range of strategies to help you cope with pressure.
- Recognizing your thoughts and emotions – and managing them.
- Being willing to persevere when the going gets tough, but also recognizing and respecting your own limits, including what you can control and what you can't.

TIPS FOR MENTAL RESILIENCE IN ADDICTION RECOVERY

- Remain Positive, looking towards the future, thinking of essential needs from life.
- Establish realistic and achievable goals which will help you focus and

implement them without procrastination.

- Plan coping strategies without fear of failure. Ask for help where and when necessary.

- Identify your strength using SWOT (Strength, Weakness, Opportunity and Threats) Analysis.

- Learn from past experience and Introduce a positive way of thinking. Focus on the good things in your life.

- Create time to do the things you enjoy and brings you pleasure.

- Connect and build healthy relationships with your family, friends and teachers.

- Embrace change and don't dwell on the past. Channel your energy into the present to shape your future. Maintain self-care and keep healthy and fit.

Having more resilience than other varies significantly in some people. Some may have qualities that make them more resilient than others. Resilience, however, is best defined in terms of behavior and support. Behaviors can be learned and support put in place, which means that, in practice, there is a lot to put in place to help people become more resilient and completely break the chains of addiction.

CHAPTER SIX
Components of Mental Resilience

Human beings are dynamic. The decisions of human being are guided by mental and affective domain before the physical operations that are manifested externally. Because humans are dynamic, their attitude, behavior and integrity can be influenced. This influence is triggered by various factors such as addiction to substance use among others. Hence, understanding the components of mental resilience as an effective tool in addiction recovery are crucial.

Self-efficacy

The ability of an individual to believe in his or her capacity to execute behaviors necessary to produce specific performance to attainments is refer to as Self-efficacy. It reflects confidence in the ability to exert control over one's behavior, motivation and social environment. These cognitive self-evaluations influence all manner of human experience, including the goals for which people strive, the amount of energy people expended toward goal achievement and likelihood of attaining particular levels of behavioral performance. Self-efficacy beliefs are hypothesized to vary depending on the human domain of functioning, and circumstances surrounding the occurrence of behavior. This also involves self-awareness in having conscious knowledge of one's personality, including strength, weakness, emotion and motivation. It also allows an individual to understand other people's perception on them.

Optimism

Every human need to be optimistic. Purpose is not achieved in the absence of optimism. Being optimistic is a driven force to fulfilling purpose in life. Hence, Optimism is a general belief that good things will happen rather than bad things in the future. Thus, optimism, as a personality trait, reflects good expectations for the future. Scientific evidence suggests that being optimistic help improves good health mentally and physically. Optimistic individuals seem able to solve problems they face more rapidly. Because optimistic individuals have positive expectations for the future, they experience less anxiety and daily problems, they experience more positive emotions and they have more life satisfaction. Thus, they suffer less depressive symptoms because they can deal with problems more strongly. Studies have shown that high levels of optimism may decrease symptoms of depression. This shows that optimism is crucial in conquering depression in withdrawal syndrome as an individual quits substance use.

Optimism helps to make it possible for people to believe that bad situation can improve by motivating them to change those situations. Example, it makes an individual to cling to treatment regimen and to seek advice, which helps to solve life problem before they spiral out of control. It also helps people to build friendship and supportive relationship, by motivating them to think that other people will like them. Having friends and social support helps to reduce the risk of addiction recovery person to have a recurrence of craving of chronic withdrawal syndrome.

Optimism affect the body at a physical level by influencing the immune system. Optimistic individuals are less vulnerable of contagious diseases that pessimistic individuals. Because people who are habitually pessimistic tend to have lower immune activities.

Adaptability

Change and growth is on the increase in today's world. Technology, transport and world affairs are driving this quickening period. Recovery from addiction expose the world differently. The individual begins to see his/her environment new. This makes is difficult to cope and regain what has been lost. Hence, to begin a new life and have a hope of facing the world again, adaptability is important.

Adaptability is the ability to modify and change your thoughts, emotions and behaviors in response to change. We are living in a period of enormous and rapid technological and scientific change and as Charles Darwin said ***"It is not the strongest of the species that survives, not the most intelligent that survives. It is the one that is the most adaptable to change."***

Adaptability is also pivotal to effective collaboration, experimentation and empowerment, because collaboration requires us to adapt our style of communication with others; experimentation requires us to adapt our mind-set to new possibilities and empowerment requires us to adapt how we see ourselves and what we can influence.

Adapting behavior starts with a deliberate change of perspective on the presenting situation, adapting how we think about things. Depending on the eye with which we are looking through at the time we will 'see' different things, we build different stories about what is happening and what our choices are. Doing this, changes how we 'feel' about things. In difficult situations, a good tip is to ask yourself what Eye you are looking through and mentally change the Eye to get a different perspective. When this adaptation takes place, breaking chains of addiction and having full restoration of livelihood is inevitable.

Emotional Intelligence

People with high **emotional intelligence** are better equipped to manage stress, cope with negative emotions, and build healthy relationships. While those with low emotional intelligence may turn to substances as a way to cope with emotional challenges, lacking the skills to navigate complex feelings. In order to Intervene with such situation, there's need to focus on developing emotional awareness and regulation which can enhance an individual's ability to resist addictive behaviors. Moreover, recognizing emotional stimulus is important in the prevention of relapse. Therapeutic approaches that will integrate emotional intelligence training can empower individuals to identify and manage stimulus, thereby reducing the likelihood of succumbing to addictive tendencies.

In addiction recovery, emotional intelligence is the ability to recognize, understand, and manage one's own emotions, as well as to empathize with the emotions of others. It helps individuals to recognize and understand their emotions, including stimulus that may lead to cravings or relapse, to effectively manage and regulate their emotions, reducing the reliance on substances as a coping mechanism. It also helps an individual to cultivate intrinsic motivation for recovery, setting and working towards meaningful goals that align with a healthier lifestyle, understand and connect with the emotions of others, fostering stronger relationships and support networks within the recovery social environment. These can help develop effective communication and interpersonal skill, crucial for navigating the complexities of relationships and seeking support during challenging times.

Fostering emotional intelligence promotes resilience and a more sustainable path toward lasting sobriety.

25

CHAPTER SEVEN
Therapies in Addiction Recovery

BEHAVIORAL THERAPY

From the perspective of cognitive-behavior theory, alcohol and drug dependence are viewed as learned behaviors that are acquired through experience. If alcohol or a drug provides certain desired results such as good feelings, reduced tension or stress and relief from emotional trauma, on repeated occasions, it may become the preferred way of achieving those results, particularly in the absence of other ways of meeting those desired results. From this point of view, the primary goals of treatment are to identify the specific needs that alcohol and drugs are being used to meet, and develop skills that provide alternative ways of meeting those needs.

Behavioral approaches emphasize observable antecedents and consequences of behavior, without making reference to internal events, such as cognitions, that can only be known by self-report. Substance use or dependence has in a way connected to Behavior and Cognition. Behavior can be triggered by friends, environment, certain testimonies or events. While cognition can be triggered by thoughts, emotion or feelings. These are reason why Behavioral therapy is considered vital in the management of addiction or substance dependence. One of the major way to deal with this, is through Coping-Skills Training.

Coping-Skill Training approach does not attempt to reduce the impact of triggers. Rather, it accepts triggers as a given and seeks to train alternative responses to them, so that a person will have several ways of coping with the occurrence of a trigger situation, in place of drinking/drug use. With sufficient practice of the alternative coping skills, it becomes increasingly likely that they will be utilized when a trigger situation arises, rather than resorting to drinking or drug use. Deficits in skills for coping with the antecedents and consequences of drinking/drug use are considered to be a major contributor to the development and maintenance of addictive behavior.

Coping-Skill Training: Heavy drinkers and drug abusers may use alcohol or drugs to cope with certain problems in their lives. Through repeated experience of the apparent short term benefits of drinking or drug use, they may become the preferred way of coping, especially in the absence of other coping skills. If alcohol or drugs are the only way a person has to cope with certain things, then he/she is psychologically dependent upon them. Such a person has no choice, to drink or use a drug if those needs are to be met. Skills training can be used to teach coping behaviors not currently in a client's repertoire, to refresh or enhance deficient behaviors, and to identify and reduce inhibiting factors. In all cases, adequate practice of skills is essential, both during sessions and as homework, so that clients become 'fluent' in the skills and are able to apply them fairly easily when the appropriate circumstances arise, without having to do a lot of thinking about the various steps involved or figuring out how to apply them.

Managing thoughts and cravings for use:

Thoughts about drinking or drug use, and cravings, are common among people recovering from substance use or addiction. Client are taught a number of skills for managing thoughts and cravings, including challenging them, recalling unpleasant experiences that resulted from using, anticipating the benefits of not using, distracting oneself, delaying the decision whether or not to use, leave the situation and seeking support. They are also asked to imagine various high-risk situations, and practice coping with the thoughts and cravings that might accompany them.

Anger management:

In addiction recovery, anger is a very common antecedent to alcohol/drug use. Clients are taught about the warning signs of anger, both external and internal signs, so they can identify them early and begin to manage them before anger grows strong and becomes harder to control. Skills for managing anger include the use of calm-down phrases, identifying aspects of a situation that are provoking anger, and considering options that might help to resolve the situation.

Negative thinking:

This is another common high-risk situation. In addiction recovery, it paramount to teach an individual to recognize various types of negative thinking habits that may occur automatically. Skills for managing negative thoughts include substituting positive thoughts or feelings, thought stopping, and positive self-talk.

Decision-making:

Sometimes clients end up relapsing after a series of incremental steps that gradually led them ever closer to craving and then to actually using their substance of choice. Decision-making training can help clients think ahead to the possible consequences of all the decisions they make, even the ones that are seemingly irrelevant to substance use, to increase the likelihood that they will anticipate, and act upon, the relative risks associated with various decision options.

Drink/drug refusal:

Knowing how to cope with offers to use alcohol or drugs is an important skill for the majority of chemically dependent clients because such offers are fairly common. Clients are taught to say 'no' convincingly without giving a double message, to suggest an alternative activity that does not involve substance use, to change the subject to a different topic of conversation, and if the other person persists, to ask him/her not to offer alcohol or drugs any more. With considerable practice of this skill, clients should be able to respond quickly and convincingly when these situations arise.

Enhancing social support network:

Support from others often makes people feel more confident about their ability to cope with problems. Given the number of life problems caused or exacerbated by substance abuse, a good social support network can enhance the chances of coping effectively. Other coping skills includes: Refusing requests, General social skills, Intimate relationships, Handling criticism, and problem-solving.

MOTIVATIONAL ENHANCEMENT THERAPY

Motivation is a critical element of behavior change that predicts client abstinence and reductions in substance use. You cannot give clients motivation, but you can help them identify their reasons and need for change and facilitate planning for change. In order to successfully achieve the treatment of substance dependence or addiction, there is need acknowledge motivation as a multidimensional, fluid state during which people make difficult changes to health-risk behaviors, like substance misuse.

Motivation is a key to behavioral change in addiction recovery. It is a complex construct with evolving meanings. Self-Determination theory is one framework for understanding motivation and how it relates to behavior changes. It suggests that people inherently want to engage in activities that meet their need for autonomy, competency i.e. self-efficacy and relatedness such as having close personal relationships. There are two kinds of motivation: Intrinsic motivation e.g. desires, needs, values, and goals and Extrinsic motivation e.g. social influences, external rewards, and consequences.

Providing a supportive relational context that promotes client autonomy and competence, enhances intrinsic motivation, which helps clients internalize extrinsic motivational rewards, and supports behavior change. Motivation includes clients' internal desires, needs, and values. It also includes external pressures, demands that influence clients and their perceptions about the risks and benefits of engaging in substance use behaviors.

It is important to note that in addiction recovery, motivation is a part of human experience. No one is totally unmotivated. It is accessible and can be enhanced at many points in the change process. Historically, in addiction treatment it was thought that clients had to "hit bottom" or experience terrible, irreparable consequences of their substance misuse to become ready to change. Research now shows that counselors can help clients identify and explore their desire, ability, reasons, and need to change substance use behaviors; this effort enhances motivation and facilitates movement toward change.

CREATIVE-BASED THERAPY

Within our society, the abuse of alcohol and drugs presents broad consequences that affect every individual on some level. However, alternative treatment models have been introduced within many drug and alcohol treatment centers as a therapy in addiction recovery. Art therapy, active within multiple aspects of the mental health field, has been utilized for several decades now as a treatment modality with individuals suffering from addictions. Creative arts therapists can be especially effective in helping clients overcome denial and shame, allowing them to admit their life is out of control.

Creative Art Therapy is a session that helps individual explore their emotion and improve mental health. It helps patient or client learn about themselves through artistic expression. This is to allow client or patient themselves in imaginative and non-verbal ways. There are various ways in which this therapy can be achieved. This can be through ***Pro-Con Collage, Music, Check-in Drawings, Painting, Hypothetical Greeting Card etc***. These forms of therapy help to promote self-reflection, resolve emotional conflicts, decrease denial to addiction, reduce anxiety, improve self-esteem, encourage self-awareness and reinforces commitment to recovery.

In addiction recovery, creative art therapy provides opportunity for an individual to express his or her past experiences, thoughts and emotion in a positive manner and meaningful way. It is also important for people suffering from a condition known as Alexithymia, in which people cannot describe their emotions or identify them.

CHAPTER EIGHT
Treatment Options

DETOXIFICATIION

Detoxification seeks to minimize the physical harm or adverse effect caused by addicted substance or drugs. It is one of the major treatment plan in managing patient with who is substance or drug dependent. Detoxification is a set of interventions aimed at managing intoxications and withdrawal. It denotes the clearing of toxin from the body of an individual who is acutely intoxicated or dependent on substance of abuse. It is also a medical intervention that manage an individual safely through the process of withdrawal.

Detoxification may prevent potentially life-threatening complications that might appear if the patient were left untreated. At the same time, detoxification is a form of palliative care (reducing the intensity of a disorder) for those who want to become abstinent or who must observe mandatory abstinence as a result of hospitalization or legal involvement. Finally, for some patients it represents a point of first contact with the treatment system and the first step to recovery. Treatment/rehabilitation, on the other hand, involves a constellation of ongoing therapeutic services ultimately intended to promote recovery for substance abuse patients. It involves some essential components as:

- **Evaluation** entails testing for the presence of substances of abuse in the bloodstream, measuring their concentration, and screening for co-occurring mental and physical conditions. Evaluation also includes a comprehensive assessment of the patient's medical and psychological conditions and social situation to help determine the appropriate level of treatment following detoxification. Essentially, the evaluation serves as the basis for the initial substance abuse treatment plan once the patient has been withdrawn successfully.

- **Stabilization** includes the medical and psychosocial processes of assisting the patient through acute intoxication and withdrawal to the attainment of a medically stable, fully supported, substance free state. This often is done with the assistance of medications, though in some approaches to detoxification no medication is used. Stabilization includes familiarizing patients with what to expect in the treatment milieu and the role in treatment and recovery.

- **Fostering** the patient's entry into treatment involves preparing the patient for entry into substance abuse treatment by stressing the importance of following through with the complete substance abuse treatment continuum of care. For patients who have demonstrated a pattern of completing detoxification services and then failing to engage in substance abuse treatment, a written treatment contract may encourage entrance into a continuum of substance abuse treatment and care. This contract, which is not legally binding, is voluntarily signed by patients when they are stable enough to do so at the beginning of treatment. In it, the patient agrees to participate in a continuing care plan, with details and contacts established prior to the completion of detoxification.

REHABILITATION

Addiction is a process that has many negative consequences and negatively affects individuals, families and societies. Addiction recovery, has made it difficult for people to fully adapt or cope with the new world and engage in their daily activities as usual. Some lost their job, families and other social aspect of life as addict and needed to recover all and start a new life. Rehabilitation aims to achieve recovery which includes both the concepts of hope and hardship, support social integration and focusing on helping people make their own free choices and maximize the quality of life that helps people feel good.

Rehabilitation is a set of interventions designed to optimize functioning and reduce disability in individuals with health conditions in interaction with their environment (WHO). It involves extensive therapy, which aims to rectify drug-seeking behaviors, instill better coping mechanisms, and teach important relapse prevention skill. As part of ongoing recovery, various outlets of aftercare provide individual with long-term support and continued relapse prevention opportunities.

An effective rehabilitation service should cover health, social security, education and job related applications based on human rights, ensuring active participation of individuals in treatment of addiction, improving their social functioning and reducing their social threat is important.

Treatment/rehabilitation includes an ongoing, continual assessment of the patient's physical, psychological, and social status, as well as analyzing of environmental risk factors that may be contributing to substance use and the identification of immediate relapse triggers, including prevention strategies for coping with them. It also includes the delivery of primary medical care and psychiatric care, if necessary, to help the patient abstain from substance use and minimize the physical harm caused by it. Ultimately, the goal of rehabilitation is to attain a higher level of social functioning by reducing risk factors, enhancing protective factors, and thus decreasing the possibility of relapse, ensuring that individual as a hope for living a successful life again.

Maintenance includes the continuation of counseling and support specified in the treatment plan, refinement and strengthening of strategies to avoid relapse, and engagement in ongoing relapse prevention, aftercare, and/or domiciliary care.

CHAPTER NINE

Way-Out

COMMUNITY INVOLVEMENT INITIATIVE

By Involving community members, prevention systems are learned firsthand from individuals and community members about substance use problems and social determinants that influence behavioral health. Community involvement brings together the skills, knowledge, and experiences of diverse groups to create and implement solutions that work for all members of the community. Development of an effective community-based prevention strategy to address substance use depends on assessment and engagement at the community level, which requires community voice concerning how substance use affects individuals, families, neighborhoods, and community sectors e.g. child welfare, health care, law enforcement.

Community involvement requires trust and begins by gathering the community members or assembling a group of community members. Relationships and the trust upon which they are built need to be in place. Authentic community involvement efforts recognize that there may be distrust in the community. This helps in dispelling myths or misconception about addiction recovery as members shares traumatic history and their victory over certain challenges and gained total recovery without relapse.

In community involvement, organizations and individuals are brought together around a shared purpose, such as prevention of substance use, and shared decision-making and equity among participants. It focuses on making a difference in the community and having an impact on the identified problem which is intended to move communities toward desired outcomes. All participants are valued for their contributions. Information and resources are shared among community members and stakeholders to advance outcomes and build community capacity.

FAMILY ROLE (Family Therapy)

Addiction puts family members under a great deal of stress, disrupting routines and causing unsettling or even frightening experiences. As a result, family members develop unhealthy coping strategies as they strive to maintain equilibrium in the household. The family unit becomes a fragile and dysfunctional system, and this often unwittingly contributes to the addiction as the family adopts destructive behaviors as a result of it. As with any recovery, it is sometimes necessary and helpful to gather information, to better understand what others are seeing or feeling. For a family, information and help must be sought for the whole family before the recovery can be complete. Information and understanding may be all that are necessary to bring about recovery, but a specialist might also be necessary, since there may be grief and loss to overcome in the process. The person with the addiction is the center, and though the key to alcohol and drug addiction recovery, not necessarily the most important in family recovery. The "world" revolves around this person, causing the addict to become the center of attention. Everyone in the family has a major role to play. As the roles are defined, the others unconsciously take on the rest of the roles to complete the balance after the problem has been introduced. The parts played by family members lead to codependency. Members make decisions concerning what the other person needs. Codependency leads to aversion and lack of self-orientation in a situation where an addiction is present. Ultimately people become the part they are playing. The goal in alcohol and drug addiction recovery is to bring each member as a whole into a situation where the problems can be dealt with. Individual talents and abilities should be integrated into the situation, allowing emotional honesty about the situation, without guilt or punishment.

Family therapy is a fundamental part of a high-quality treatment program. Family therapy addresses dysfunction in the family system and helps family members understand the interdependent nature of that system and work to replace unhealthy thoughts, attitudes and behaviors with healthier ones. Productive change comes about through improving communication skills, exploring relationship patterns among family members and working to restore trust and rebuild damaged relationships. Family behavior therapy is an outpatient treatment that's been shown to reduce drug and alcohol use in both adults and adolescents, and it improves family functioning by addressing a variety of issues. Co-occurring problems like depression, unemployment, conduct disorders and child mistreatment must be managed in order to restore optimal family functioning.

CHAPTER TEN

New Resolution

As individual gain total recovery from addiction without relapse, he/she faces the new world. In or to cope with new life and enjoy effective rehabilitation process, it is important to be determinant in setting new goals for a better life. This determination in setting new goals, and optimism preoccupies the mind, filling every vacuum for negative thoughts and other addiction triggers. This phase is called the "New Resolution".

Resolution is a commitment an individual's make to themselves to improve their lives. Which can be adopting healthier habits, pursuing new skills, or fostering better relationships. These often reflect our desire for positive change and fulfilling purpose. The concept of resolution has evolved over time. It has pass beyond cultural and religious practices, and has now encompass physical wellbeing, mental health, career aspiration and personal/social relationship. Embracing change and self-improvement can happen at any time, and it is essential to view resolutions as a dynamic process, allowing for adjustments and flexibility as circumstances evolve.

One significant change in the approach to resolutions involves setting realistic and achievable goals, recognizing the importance of incremental progress. This increases the likelihood of success and fosters a positive mindset. Many individuals are recognizing the importance of mental health and incorporating practices such as meditation, gratitude journaling, and stress management into their resolutions. This holistic approach reflects a growing awareness of the interconnectedness between mental and physical health.

What Resolutions Entails.

Resolution entails diverse of self-improvement skills not just to resolve on not taking drugs or harmful substance. Below are some vital Tips on embracing the change and making the new resolution:

- Resolve to adapt or adhere to Behavioral, Cognitive and Enhancement Therapy regimen.

- Embrace and implement coping skill. Get a skill and build yourself in it.

- Resolve to avoid triggers such as places, friends and substance.

- Accept new friends and build good interpersonal relationship. Sit with family members and ask questions where necessary.

- Voice your emotions or feeling to them and express emotions in art or creativity.

- Embrace rehabilitation process, and if there's still detox management, adhere to it.

- Be optimistic and not pessimistic. Get into the future and break the chains of addiction and relapse.

REFERENCES

Jebraeili H, Habib M, Nazemi A. (2019) Mediating role of resilience and tendency to addiction regarding the effect of gender on substance use. J Research and Health 9(3): 236-245.

Rebecca Graber, et'l (2015), Psychological resilience: *State of knowledge and future research agendas.* Working Paper 425.

Kapıkıran, Ş., & Acun-Kapıkıran, N. (2016). Optimism and psychological resilience in relation to depressive symptoms in university students: *Examining the mediating role of self-esteem. Educational Sciences:* Theory & Practice, 16, 2087–2110.

Ronald M. Kadden, Ph.D. (2002), Cognitive-Behavior Therapy for Substance Dependence: Coping Skills Training, Farmington, CT 06030-3944.

Building your own resilience, Health and well-being. skillsforcare.org.uk 2016.

Resilience and Mental health. Health Minds Resource Pack. 2023

Sarrionandia A, Ramos-Díaz E, and Fernández-Lasarte O. (2018) Resilience as a Mediator of Emotional Intelligence and Perceived Stress: *A Cross-Country Study. Frontiers in Psychology.* 9:2653. doi: 10.3389/fpsyg.2018.02653

WorkingWell Ltd, London, 2019; Wellbeing "Health Habits" Adaptability.

Ayşegül Y.A, Fulya A.G (2021); An Effective Rehabilitation Center Model for Drug Addiction. *Dergisi-International Journal of Society Research.* DOI: 10.26466/opus.832144.

Marilyn Herie, et'l (2010). Addiction, an information guide. Centre for *Addiction and Mental Health.* 3973d / 05-2010 / pm043.

Brian J. Horay (2006); Moving Towards Gray: Art Therapy and Ambivalence in Substance Abuse Treatment Art Therapy: *Journal of the American Art Therapy Association*, 23(1) pp. 14-22.

Jim Orford (2023); Problem Gambling and Other Behavioral Addictions. *Foresight Brain Science, Addiction and Drugs project.*

Center for Substance Abuse Treatment. Detoxification and Substance Abuse Treatment. *Treatment Improvement Protocol* (TIP) Series, No. 45. HHS Publication No. (SMA) 15-4131. Rockville, MD: Center for Substance Abuse Treatment, 2006.

The Science of Addiction. *National Institute on Drug Abuse.* 2014.

Enhancing Motivation for Change in Substance Use Disorder Treatment. *Substance Abuse and mental Health Administration.* 2019; 1-877-SAMHSA-7 (1-877-726-4727).

Kathy Bettinardi-Angres and d Daniel H. Angres, (2023); Understanding the Disease of Addiction. *Journal of Nursing Regulation.* Vol. 1(2).

Substance Abuse and Mental Health Services Administration (SAMHSA). Community Engagement: *An Essential Component of an Effective and Equitable Substance Use Prevention System.* SAMHSA Publication No. PEP22-06-01-005. Rockville, MD: National Mental Health and Substance Use Policy Laboratory. Substance Abuse and Mental Health Services Administration, 2022.

ABOUT THE AUTHOR

About The Author Godwin George Godwin George is a Profession Nurse registered with the Nursing and Midwifery Council of Nigeria. He is an entrepreneur, a content creator and digital marketer. He is passionate about reaching out to people through his health books with amazing contents. He has written health Articles/Blog post and other amazing books like "Maintaining Good health" The Eye On Screen" and few others. He is the CEO of Green Pasture Health Support Initiative, currently residing in Nigeria and working with Global Alliance for Vaccine Initiative under Primary Health Care Development Agency Niger State, Nigeria.